# Animals
## EVERY CHILD SHOULD KNOW

RUDOLF
FREUND

PRESERVE OUR
WILDLIFE

LYNX
GRAY SQUIRREL
CHIPMUNK
RED FOX
PORCUPINE
OPOSSUM
RABBIT
WOODCHUCK
FIELD MOUSE
OTTER
BARN OWL
SKUNK
RACCOON
MOLE
TORTOISE
BEAVER

# Animals

## EVERY CHILD SHOULD KNOW

The Big Book of Animals Every Child Should Know

*Text by* DENA HUMPHREYS *Pictures by* RUDOLF FREUND

1977 PRINTING

ISBN: 0-448-00324-4 (Trade Edition)
ISBN: 0-448-03670-8 (Library Edition)

GROSSET & DUNLAP    *Publishers*    NEW YORK

# LYNX

THE lynx's paws leave furry, blurry tracks which you might see in country places after a fresh snowfall. But you're not apt to see the lynx himself. He doesn't choose to be where people are. Instead, he likes to roam the far wild woods and always do exactly as he pleases. He won't make friends with anyone at all, excepting his own family. He's really a wild cat, and "wildcat" is what people often call him.

The wildcat is bigger and stronger than a tame cat. His coat is long and thick and soft. It comes in a pale grayish-tannish shade sprinkled with small dark smudges. Around his chin he wears a ruff that makes his face look like a sunflower, and tufts of long hair decorate his ears. At night, his beautiful big eyes shine like the headlights of a car, and he can see in the dark when he goes hunting. He has sharp claws, but he keeps them pulled up inside his paws, except for fighting or for climbing trees. He likes to climb. He's a fierce fighter too, so fierce that other creatures never quarrel with him. A fighting wildcat spits and snarls and yowls. He makes a lot of noise when he's angry.

The wildcat's kittens love to play just as tame kittens do. They jump and roll and pounce, and sharpen their small claws by scratching trees. But one thing that they never do is chase their tails. They never twitch the tips when they're excited, or swish them angrily. They can't, because they haven't enough tail to swish.

There seem to be wildcats of one kind or another all around the world. Of course, the ones that live up north are furriest — they even have long hair between their toes. All of them make their homes in lonely, sheltered places where they feel very sure they won't be found.

# GRAY SQUIRREL

THE gray squirrel's tail is just as long as he is, and floats behind him like a smoky cloud. When he sits up on his hind legs he holds it neatly curved against his back, with the tip curling outward. It looks extremely handsome, and it's useful too, helping to balance him. He can sit on some high branch of a tall tree and never worry about falling off. Besides, he has long-fingered paws instead of round pads like a cat's or a dog's, so it's easy for him to jump and scurry through the treetops.

Among the branches far above our heads the squirrel has a secret nest. But he doesn't stay up there all the time. He can scamper straight down a tree trunk head first, trailing his fine, fluffy tail behind him. He goes so fast, he seems to ripple, and his claws make a scratchy noise against the bark. On the ground, he hunts for nuts and acorns. When he finds one he turns it round and round in his front paws, choosing a place to start gnawing the shell with his sharp, strong teeth.

Although nuts are the squirrel's favorite food, he never stuffs himself too full of them. He eats only as many as he needs, then hides the rest down under rocks and leaves, or in a hollow stump, or else digs a hole and buries them. Then, on some wintry day when all the food is gone, he'll dig them up and have a feast.

# CHIPMUNK

THE chipmunk doesn't wash before his meals as you do. He thinks it's nicer to wash afterward. He scrubs his face, starting behind the ears. He licks his red-brown back and his white front. He holds his lovely tail between his paws and combs and fluffs it with his teeth and tongue. He eats and washes many times a day and so, of course, he's always neat and clean. Besides, the dark stripes running down his head and back make him look stylish.

Sometimes the chipmunk's head seems wider than his body. That's when his cheeks are stuffed so full of nuts that you feel sure he's just about to burst. He doesn't, though. He stuffs in still one more and scampers off to his snug little home. But he's not really greedy. He's only laying in supplies for the long winter ahead.

All summer long the chipmunk works so he can rest in winter. He digs himself a cozy hole under a tree or maybe deep among some rocks. There he stores things he likes to eat — nuts and acorns, berries and seeds and grain. When the cold weather comes, he goes to sleep down at the bottom of his hole. He rolls himself into a ball, wrapping his tail over his nose for warmth. Once in a while he uncurls himself and has a bite to eat. Then, if the sun is warm and no wind is blowing, he may step outside for a breath of air. But mostly he just sleeps.

Though he's so small, the chipmunk's quick and brave, and always wants to know what's going on. Often he lives near people, hoping that they will give him food. If you put peanuts in the grass or on the step, he'll eat the first one that he finds, holding it daintily in his tiny paws and nibbling fast. The rest he'll tuck into his cheeks to carry home. Then he'll come back looking for more. If you're quiet and don't try to stroke him, someday he'll take a nut from your hand.

# RED FOX

OF course the red fox isn't really red like a tomato or geranium. He's a bright reddish orange-brown all tipped in black, and he may have a dash of white trimming too. His ears are often black. So are his slender paws, his thin, sharp nose, and sometimes even his surprising tail. Though he himself is sleek and slim, his tail is long and full and bushy. People call it his brush, but he can't brush his coat with it, of course. He has to use his tongue for that, as dogs do.

The fox is hardly larger than a cat, but he makes up for being small by being swift and clever. He's sly and full of tricks, and that's what "foxy" means.

Foxes aren't fierce, but they're not friendly either. They like to roam the woods and fields alone, or be at home with their families. The fox's home is a secret cave dug in a bank of earth. There the cubs huddle cozily while the father and mother go hunting. The babies take long naps. They know they mustn't step outside unless their mother is with them. Sometimes she takes them to frisk in the sun, guarding them while they roll and jump in the tall grass. They pounce on grasshoppers and snap at butterflies. By and by, she shows them where to catch frogs and fish and other little creatures when they're hungry. They like to eat fruit too.

Different kinds of foxes live in different parts of the world, and they come in different colors. There are many of them, and yet you rarely see one, because they're clever about keeping hidden. If you should find a fox in a zoo, his shining gray-green eyes will stare at you as though you were not there. He looks wise, and you can tell that he knows lots of secrets.

# PORCUPINE

IF you stuck a big black pincushion full of white knitting needles, it would be rather like a porcupine. His quills are sharper than knitting needles, though, and tipped with black. They're light and hollow, like the stem of a feather with the feathery part stripped off. They seem to point every which way, as the petals of a chrysanthemum do after a storm. Quills grow all over the top of him, even on his ears and tail, but there are none on his snubby face. He's black as coal, and his round, shining eyes are blacker still.

The porcupine is not fierce or strong or quick, so he needs his quills to keep harmful creatures away. Some people think he can shoot them out of his skin like arrows. He can't, but when he's frightened or angry he bristles and shakes himself, scattering loose quills around. He doesn't mind shedding them, because new ones keep growing out through his black fur to take their place. The quills have tiny hooks along the ends to make them stick in things. Of course they hurt, and no one ever tries to pat a porcupine. With his prickly tail he will slap at an enemy who comes too close, and he always sleeps curled up like a big chestnut burr.

The porcupine lumbers about slowly and awkwardly, with his head near the ground. His toes turn inward, and his claws are curved. That helps him to climb trees. He goes way up, hunting the nicest leaves to eat. With his front teeth he rips off the rough outside layer of bark and nibbles the green, juicy bark beneath.

If you should meet a porcupine in the woods, he'd slowly go about his business, maybe rattling his quills a bit to warn you to go about yours.

# OPOSSUM

JUST for fun, did you ever pretend to be asleep when you were really wide awake? That's called "playing possum." But the possum doesn't do it for fun. He does it when he hopes no one will notice him. If you should come upon one in the woods, he'd curl up in a ball and stay quite still until you went away. He's only the size of a cat, he can't run very fast, and he's not fierce. So the best thing for him to do when he suspects that danger is near is to "play possum." If you passed by while he was up a tree he'd feel much safer.

Possums are whitish gray with bright black eyes, pink noses and dark, forward-pointing ears set low down on their heads. Most of their fur is short and thick, but they have long fur scattered over them besides. Their bare, gray tails help them climb trees, curling round branches like an extra hand. Their hind paws are rather like hands too, since they have thumbs to hold onto things with.

When the mother possum goes looking for grasshoppers and grubs and beetles and fruit and all the many things she likes to eat, she doesn't leave her babies by themselves. She takes them with her, clinging to her back. They wrap their tails round hers to make sure that they won't fall off. Sometimes she has quite a large family, and they soon grow too big for her to carry. Then the babies learn to scramble among the branches all alone and search for food.

Of course, the possum's real name is opossum, but that seems rather troublesome to say, so hardly anybody calls him that.

# RABBIT

RABBITS are soft. They have large, gentle eyes and wiggly noses and small white tails that look like powder puffs. Some people call them "cottontails."

Wild rabbits live in secret homes along the edges of the woods. They dig deep holes in the earth to keep their babies warm and safe in, while they're small. The grown-up rabbits hop about the meadows, sniffing to find the tastiest plants to eat. Their eyes are watchful and their long ears turn to catch sounds of danger. If something startles them, they scamper under a low-growing shrub. They like the tangled bramble thickets best, because the thorns keep other creatures out. But thorns can't scratch the rabbit through his heavy fur. His coat is grayish brown, the color of dead leaves and old dry grasses, so you scarcely see him if he lies still.

When he sits or hops the rabbit keeps his long back neatly curved. But when he runs he stretches himself out, flattening his big ears, and pushing with his strong hind legs so fast that nobody can catch him. Sometimes he's bold enough to feast in people's gardens, because he especially loves lettuce and parsley and spinach and carrots and cabbage and herbs.

If you should meet a rabbit, or even see a rabbit's footprints in the snow you can be sure that there are others near, because rabbits have enormous families.

# WOODCHUCK

IN autumn, when the air grows chill, we're apt to feel quite lively. The woodchuck is different. Cold weather makes him lazy. By and by, he feels so drowsy that he crawls into his home, which is a hole dug deep down in the ground. There he curls up, alone or with his family and maybe a few friends, and falls sound asleep. When the woodchuck sleeps, his body doesn't stay warm and cozy as yours does. It cools off fast, but his thick fur and the nice layer of fat under his skin keep him from freezing through and through. Winter comes, and the earth gets colder and colder. So does the woodchuck, but he doesn't mind. He doesn't even know he's cold, because he can't feel anything at all. He sleeps so hard, he scarcely breathes. Even his heart beats slowly, and nothing except warmth can wake him up.

Months later, when the ground begins to thaw, the woodchuck starts to take large breaths again. Then his heart beats faster and his muscles unstiffen. Soon he wants to stretch and move around and have a look about him. He climbs out of his hole, sits up on his hind legs, blinks at the light and wiggles his black nose. People believe he wakes up on February 2nd, which is called "Groundhog Day," as "groundhog" is another of the woodchuck's names. They say that if he sees his shadow on that day he'll go back to sleep, and that means there'll be six more weeks of winter. Of course that isn't really true, but it *is* true that woodchucks seem to know when spring has come to stay.

The woodchuck wakes up very thin indeed, and he sets right to work at getting fat. It isn't hard, because he eats so many different things — roots and twigs, buds and grasses, nuts and seeds, berries and other fruit, and insects. Some of the animals that rest all winter in their secret homes lay in a large supply of food. The wood-chuck doesn't. He stores food inside himself, so that by the time the first frost arrives he waddles just a little as he walks.

# WHITE-FOOTED FIELD MOUSE

SOMETIMES the field mouse eats queer things that you and I would never dream of eating — candles and soap, for instance, which would make us sick. Of course, he doesn't find candles and soap in the woods and fields where he's supposed to live. But mice are bold in spite of being small. They come right into people's houses and make themselves at home. They like barns too, where there's warm hay and lots of seed and grain, and that's why farmers usually keep a cat. Cats are fond of a mouse for dinner. Wise mice know this, and so they stay away.

The field mouse is much handsomer than the dusty-brown city mouse. His coat is steely gray with a white shirt front, his eyes and ears are large, and he has quivery whiskers. Since he is busiest at night, he needs those big ears and long whiskers to help him hear and feel things in the dark. He's neat and pleasant looking, so you might suppose that people would be glad to have him share their homes. But he's a nuisance, really. He only eats candles and soap when he can't get more delicious things such as cheese and chocolate and bacon and crackers and cake. It isn't any fun to find that a mouse has nibbled the cookies, or that he's made a nest inside your favorite sofa, or that his strong teeth have gnawed a hole right through a kitchen shelf. The nicest mice are those that stay outdoors where they belong.

It's queer that people say "quiet as a mouse," because a mouse is not so very quiet. Of course, mice *can* be quiet and they sometimes are, especially when they're frightened. But in old country houses you often hear them squeak and scamper. Some mice can even sing — not tunes, of course. They sing a small, high note that just goes on and on, and people think they do it because they're happy.

# OTTER

THE otter looks cheerful. He likes to play. He loves to slide down waterfalls. He teases other otters to play with him. They chase and wrestle under water, thrashing and splashing with their long, strong tails, or dart along the stream so fast that your eyes can barely follow them.

When the otter is tired he scrambles up onto the shore. His paddle feet make a moist, squishy noise, and water drips from his sleek, glistening body. But then he shakes himself, spraying the wetness off him in a diamond cloud, and after that his fur looks like deep velvet. He suns himself, rubbing against the rocks as if to comb his splendid dark brown coat. On his head the paler underfur shows through and makes his face seem frosty. It's a snub-nosed face with small, neat, streamlined ears. His whiskers bristle, and his eyes are bright.

By and by, the otter feels rested and wants to romp again, so he slips into the cool stream to twist and turn and roll and tumble beneath the sliding water. If he's hungry he catches a fish and carries it onto the shore to eat. He's so clever and skillful that in China people train otters to do their fishing for them.

Otters live in the faraway wild woods, by lakes and streams. They make hidden nests for their babies, lining their homes with soft, dry grass and leaves. And they're so shy that people seldom see them. But in zoos, otters grow tame. When the keeper brings fish they lope at his heels like big, eager dogs. To run, they have to arch their backs, because their legs are short and their bodies are long.

Otters are full of fun. Even the old ones don't behave in a dull, serious way. In fact, they never do seem to grow up.

# BARN OWL

BY day the barn owl likes to stay hidden in a hollow tree or some snug hole among the rocks. He sleeps, or else keeps his eyes almost closed because the sunshine dazzles him. As darkness falls, he opens his eyes wide. They're large and round and black and glowing gold. He perches on a branch and stares and stares, feeling awake and hungry. When night has come, he hunts for mice and fish and even snakes, swooping through the dim forest on soft, silent wings. He can see well by starlight.

The owl has a flat face, a round head, and a neck that doesn't show, because his feathers cover it. His eyes don't move, and to look at things he has to turn his head. He turns it till it seems to be on backward, then brings it so fast to the other side that you can't see him do it. It looks as though his head went round and round.

There are owls all over the world — little ones like sparrows, big ones nearly two feet tall, and all the sizes in between. Most of them are brown or gray, with handsome stripes, and some have tufts of feathers on their heads shaped like a cat's ears, or else like tiny horns. Those that live where it's hot go barelegged as most birds do. The rest wear feathers even on their feet. Some make an ugly screeching noise. Others call "Whoo-hoo-hoo-hoooo," from the dark forest, and on a still night the soft, lonely sound can be heard miles away.

Barn owls live near farms, and farmers should be glad to have them there, because they eat the rats and mice. Most of the other kinds live in the quiet woods.

Unless he's hunting, the owl seldom moves. Even a young and foolish one can sit so still and stare so hard that people like to call him "wise old owl."

# SKUNK

SKUNKS don't mind the smell of skunk. All other creatures do, including you. Yet it's not bad when it's quite far away. Often, in the country on summer nights, there comes a whiff of something queer and sharp, like nothing you've ever smelled before. Then you know that somewhere a skunk has felt annoyed.

Skunks can give off this smell suddenly whenever they want to, and so they're not afraid of anything at all. They never need to run or fight, so they're not quarrelsome and they're not shy. They're naturally peaceful and bother nobody unless they're bothered first. If you should meet one in the woods, it would be wisest to walk quietly to a safe distance, because the skunk might feel worried if a stranger came too close. And if he did, you would be very, very sorry.

Since the skunk never has to hide, his coloring doesn't match woodsy things like rocks and trees. He has a gorgeous coat and doesn't care at all if people see him.

His long, thick fur is black and glossy. Down his back two sharp white stripes spread out like waves behind a boat. He has a white cap too, and a white line right down the middle of his small black face. He's handsome, neat and clean, and useful too, eating the pests that ruin the farmer's crops.

Baby skunks can't throw a scent till they're quite grown up. For safety's sake their mother keeps them close beside her when she prowls and putters through the woods and fields, searching for food. Often she hunts at night. Sometimes at dawn or dusk you'll see a family on parade. The babies' small striped backs bob along behind the mother's big one, and all their fluffy white-tipped tails gaily stand straight up in the air.

Once in a while a family of skunks will choose to live by someone's wood-shed or under somebody's porch. Then, if the people in the house are always thoughtful and polite, the skunks won't smell or do a bit of harm. They're really rather friendly as long as nobody gets in their way.

# RACCOON

THE raccoon looks much bigger than he is, because he's made mostly of thick, deep fur that stands as straight as long grass in a field. It's pepper-and-salt color, neatly trimmed with black. He has black rings around his tail, and a black pattern on his face that makes him seem surprised and puzzled even when he's not puzzled or surprised at all. There are dark patches round his eyes.

The raccoon's paws aren't made for walking only. He has thin, curling fingers to help him climb trees, and in the daytime he's apt to sleep high up in a forked branch. When twilight comes he scrambles down and prowls for food. He will eat almost anything — nuts and berries, and minnows and crabs, beetles, carrots and corn, and ever so much else besides. Often he'll snoop round someone's kitchen porch, hoping to find a scrap of bacon or a bun or a bit of candy. He pokes about with his sharp nose and his black fingers, and scratches things with his useful claws.

The raccoon is quite queer about his meals. He likes them to be very soft and wet, so he carries his food to a stream and dips it in the water. Then he rubs and kneads it with his paws, like dough, before he eats. Pet raccoons always have to have a water pan to wash their food in.

Someday, if you go for a walk in the woods and are very lucky, you may see a raccoon, especially when daylight begins to fade. That's when raccoons feel wakeful and hungry and start searching for things to eat. They live all over North America, wherever there are lots of trees and not too many people.

# MOLE

THE mole is like a nice fat frankfurter wrapped up in dark-gray velvet. In front he has a little pointed nose, in back he has a little pointed tail, and he appears to have no face at all. His mouth is underneath. His ears are only small holes in his fur, and his eyes are so tiny that you'd never know they're there. Of course he can't see well with eyes like that, but then, he doesn't need to. In fact, large eyes would merely bother him. He spends his time burrowing underground where there's no light to see by, and if he had the usual sort of face it would get quite uncomfortably full of dirt. Down there among the roots he hunts for earthworms. He likes to eat other insects too, and he has an enormous appetite. His wide front paws grow close beside his nose. They're strong and work like shovels. Have you ever seen a mountain range about three inches high spoiling somebody's smooth green lawn? That's the mole's tunnel, and it shows you just where he's been.

Sometimes, where the ground is hard, the mole comes up into the daylight. His legs are so short that they hardly show, but he moves fast, rippling along like a huge caterpillar in a hurry. His fur is soft and even, like a carpet. He's strong, much stronger than you think, considering he's scarcely larger than a mouse. And if he hasn't had enough to eat he can be very fierce in a small way.

When winter comes, the mole doesn't fall asleep for weeks as some animals do. He's much too hungry ever to do that. Instead, he digs down farther from the cold and keeps on finding worms and grubs in the deep earth all winter long.

# TORTOISE

THE tortoise has no fur. He has no feathers either. He has no scales as snakes and fishes do. In fact, the middle of him has no skin or bones. That's why he needs his hard, thick, bumpy shell. He can't come out of it, but he can poke his head out, and his legs, and his small pointed tail. When something frightens him, or when he's sleepy, he pulls his head backward into his neck, and then he pulls his neck backward into his shell. He pulls his legs and tail inside, too, and he can close his shell up tight, because the flat, floor part of it is jointed.

The tortoise never runs around for fun. He goes straight to wherever he wants to be, and it takes him a long time to get there. He has to heave himself up and push himself slowly forward with his stiff, scratchy claws. His claws grow out of the ends of his queer, twisted legs as though he hadn't any feet. Since he can't bend in the middle, he climbs over things clumsily like an army tank.

There are lots of different kinds of turtles and you can often find them in the woods and fields. Many have bright patterns on their shells, as though someone had painted them. If you should see one whose roof shell was rather flat instead of high and round, he wouldn't be a tortoise at all. He'd be a turtle. Turtles spend most of their time in the water. Tortoises always stay on land. They like to eat green leaves, cutting them neatly with their hard, toothless jaws.

Once you've grown up, you will stay the same size. Tortoises don't. They keep on slowly growing bigger for years. Luckily, their shells get bigger too.

# BEAVER

THE beaver is a sticky-looking creature, but that's because he's usually wet. Even when it's cold he swims and swims. He has two kinds of fur — a long, coarse, oily outside coat, and below that his underwear, finer than silk, warmer than wool, softer than velvet. The water hardly ever soaks through his skin. He can swim fast, making no splash or sound. But sometimes he lies still, watching and listening for danger, and you might mistake him for a floating log. If he hears someone coming he slaps the water hard with his peculiar tail. It's wide and flat just like a leather paddle. The noise it makes hitting the surface warns his friends. Then all the beavers in the pond roll out of sight beneath the dark water.

You see beaver houses in the north woods wherever there are lakes and streams. Each house is a round island made of mud and branches. By and by, the weather turns the house silvery gray because the beavers strip the branches clean of bark. They like to eat bark, and it's good for them.

Inside the house the beavers build a nice dry shelf to sleep on, and there the babies live while they are small. It's safe, because the door is under water so that no enemy creature can get in. To make the water deep enough to hide their door, but not to flood their shelf, the beavers build a dam down where the pond flows off into a brook. A man would take measurements and figure with pencil and paper how to make the dam. Beavers don't need to. They just know.

Each house belongs to several families and they all help each other work. Some waddle off into the woods to gnaw down trees. When a tree falls, other beavers cut off the branches, slide them to the shore and swim with them to the house or dam. They drag the branches into place, packing the spaces full of mud which they pat firm with their paws and tails. When all the building is done, they pile more wood close to the house, so they'll have enough bark to eat in winter.

The beaver has a heavy body and short legs. On land he's a dark, clumsy hump and doesn't look as clever as he is. His face is queer, with small eyes and ears, and two immense front teeth as sharp and strong as chisels. His teeth are really tools. His tail's a tool, too. He uses them a lot, and he always seems to have many things to do. No wonder people talk of being "busy as a beaver."

RUDOLF FREUND